The Wit of Golf

Compiled by
Tom Scott and
Geoffrey Cousins

with illustrations by
Paul Trevillion
and a Foreword by
Ted Ray

LESLIE FREWIN of LONDON

---

*First published 1972 by
Leslie Frewin Publishers Limited,
Five Goodwin's Court,
Saint Martin's Lane, London, WC2N 4LL*

*This book is set in Bembo,
Printed and bound in Great Britain by
R. J. Acford Ltd., Industrial Estate, Chichester, Sussex*

ISBN 85632 004 8

CONTENTS

'Fore' - word *by Ted Ray*

There is a famous painting of a little boy standing on a cushion in front of a table, behind which are sitting four or five Cromwellian-type blokes, and one of them is asking the kid: 'When did you last see your father?' Nobody has ever discovered what the little boy replied until the other day. I came across it in an old volume in a second-hand bookshop and it states clearly that the boy said: 'Looking for a brand new ball in the bushes on the sixteenth.'

Also – for your information – those aren't Cromwellians at all; it's the Green Committee.

Now, I don't know who painted that picture, but it certainly wasn't me. I *do* paint in oils, but without much success, I'm afraid. I once painted my cocker-spaniel and when my wife saw it she said: 'Oh, goody, just what I've always wanted, a Red Indian Chief.' My painting is not very good. Unfortunately, neither is my golf, but at least I can laugh at myself and my efforts. Of course, it's all in the mind. Just stand beside the first tee any Saturday morning and watch the players drive off. Look at those practice swings. Slowly back, straight left arm, wrists cocking naturally, lead down with the left side and a beautiful follow-through. They put a ball down and what happens? An excruciatingly painful drag back of the arms, a demoniacal expression on the face, a murderous chop down and up comes a divot on which you could write 'Welcome' and put on your front doorstep. The poor man then turns to his three friends and screams – 'What am I doing?', as if anyone could tell him, and even if they did he wouldn't listen. It's all the fault of the Government, of course. If they had been any good they would have done away with golf balls years ago . . .

Please don't get me wrong. I'm not suggesting that the object of the game is to walk about five miles carrying a heavy bag of clubs on a dislocated shoulder and laughing hysterically, but golf *can* be fun.

One of the most refreshing sights of recent years has been the advent of Lee Trevino, whose asides, even in the middle of a Championship, would put many so-called comedians to shame. For instance, quite recently in the vital third round of a tournament, he 'skied' a ball high into the air from the tee, dropped his club, went down on his knees and pleaded: 'Don't touch it, Lord, it's a two-stroke penalty.' What a golfer, and what a man! Incidentally, he won the Competition, which proves that a laugh or two in the middle of a round can take the edge off. Get it out of your system on the course and don't wait until you get to the nineteenth. For even there you can find it difficult to laugh on occasions, especially if you are in the company of someone with short arms and low pockets. You've met them. They keep their wallets in their trouser turn-ups!

Committee work can be fun, too. As captain of my club, I once sat with several other Cromwellians (see my second paragraph) and a young fellow came in to be interviewed for prospective membership. We asked him several questions which he answered with alacrity, and then one of our older committeemen leaned forward and said: 'Is there anything you would like to ask us?' 'Yes, there is', replied the young man, 'What's the crumpet like in the Ladies' Section?' Needless to say, he didn't get in!

Thus, I'm sure you will enjoy this book, jointly compiled by Tom Scott and Geoffrey Cousins, each of whom has given great service to the Royal and Ancient game –Tom, whose gentle Scottish voice reaches us on our car radios when the sun is blazing down and we wish that we ourselves were out on the course, and Geoffrey, with his splendid articles and vivid descriptions.

If I hadn't taken my wit into show business, I wouldn't have minded being in a job like Tom's or Geoffrey's. And if I couldn't have been one of them then I think I would like to have been a golfer.

DO YOU KNOW WHY YOU HIT SO MANY BAD SHOTS?
GOLF LESSONS
I JUST CAN'T THINK!
THAT'S RIGHT!
TREVILLION

INTRODUCTION

We suppose that any book dealing with the humour of golf must inevitably be based on the exchange of remarks between the duffer and the caddie at St Andrews. 'Golf is a funny game, don't you think, caddie?', remarked the self-conscious rabbit as he holed his fourth putt on the home green for a score of 110 under the disapproving gaze of his temporary henchman. 'Maybe it is, the way ye' play it', said the caddie, opening his uncompromising lips for the first time in the round, 'but it's no' meant to be'.

Our task is to prove that golf *is* a funny game. It is made so by those who play it, those who watch it, those who organise it, those who service it. By its very nature a round of golf is bound to contain incidents, and the most serious moment often contains the germ of laughter which explodes in the aftermath.

This collection of stories is made from a variety of sources, mainly verbal. It contains many true ones—true in the sense that they are vouched for by real people who took part in the charade or were involved as onlookers. Then there are what we might call the half-true ones, built up by *raconteurs* from dimly-remembered or carelessly-recorded facts, and losing nothing in the development. The third class of story is the truly apochryphal, fruit of the imagination and often so outrageous as to be regarded as beyond the bounds of human experience.

These divisions are mentioned only to show the diversity of our anthology, because in our view there are no clear lines of demarcation. What purports to be a true story may depend almost entirely on imaginative detail which has no basis in fact. A half-true story may be less true than it looks —or less fictional. And who shall say that truly apochryphal stories can never be related to real life?

Humour, after all, is a human experience and one of the most civilising forces in everyday existence. Its chief virtue is that to be really enjoyed it must be shared; and the possible reactions range from the quiet chuckle at the marital fireside to the exploding belly-laughs in the men's bar. Our object has been to project that humour in such a way that it can please all tastes and give offence to none.

Since even a book of wit must have a plan we have endeavoured to segregate not only the sexes but also various classes. Hence our main headings concern among others Women Golfers, Caddies, Players, Professionals, and we are not unduly apologetic about the fact that the lines of separation are not unblurred. Incidents and quotations connected with the running of golf clubs have a special section, and with the help of colleagues we have a selection of those slips of the pen and typographical tangles which occur in even the best-regulated newspaper offices.

So many stars of stage, screen and television play golf these days that any anthology of this kind would be incomplete without a collection of their experiences and sayings on the course, and in this section will also be found favourite stories contributed by our friends of the Show-Biz world.

To these friends, to our colleagues of the golfing Press, to the many correspondents who have answered our requests for stories, we offer our thanks—especially to our friend Ted Ray for his pleasant and amusing Foreword. And to the public we offer a book which, it is hoped, will enliven many a dull moment and be a constant source of entertainment.

Tom Scott

Geoffrey Cousins

Points of View

Who was the first golfer?

According to evangelist Billy Graham it was St Paul, who said that he had finished the course and fought a good fight.

* * *

Golf is a test of temper, a trial of honour, a revealer of character. It affords the chance to play the man and act the gentleman. It is a cure for care, an antidote to worry. It includes companionship with friends, social intercourse, opportunities for courtesy, kindliness and generosity to an opponent. It promotes not only physical health but moral force.

* * *

Golf increases the blood pressure, ruins the disposition, spoils the digestion, induces neurasthenia, hurts the eyes, callouses the hands, ties kinks in the nervous system, debauches morals, drives men to drink or homicide, breaks up the family, turns the ductless glands into internal warts, corrodes the pneumogastric nerve, breaks the edges off the vertebrae, induces spinal meningitis and starts angina pectoris.

* * *

Golf may be played on a Sunday, being a form of moral effort.

* * *

The game is not so easy as it seems. In the first place the terrible inertia of the ball has to be overcome.

* * *

When should a putt be conceded?

From an American magazine reporting 'National Conceded Putt Day' it appears that on this day 1,711,891 putts close to the pin were recorded, and only fourteen were conceded. The magazine in question advises that putts should be conceded only in the following circumstances:

When your opponent admits defeat and is willing to pay up.

When your opponent is two inches from the pin and three down.

When your opponent is nine feet from the hole and is your boss.

Immediately after you have holed out in one.

When your wife, who has always hated you playing golf, starts playing bridge.

* * *

Income tax has made almost as many liars out of the American people as golf has.

* * *

The one-iron is almost unplayable. You keep it in your bag the way you keep a Dostoievsky novel in your bookcase—with the vague notion that you will try it some day. In the meantime it impresses your friends.

* * *

Walter Hagen once said:

'Give me a man with big hands and big feet and no brains and I'll make a golfer of him.'

* * *

There are three main types of spin—top-spin, under-spin and lateral spin. Experts agree that under-spin is most common, but handicap golfers are inclined to disagree. Although the experts maintain it is most difficult to hit a ball with top-spin thousands of amateurs up and down the country know it is the easiest thing in the world.

* * *

Four rules for playing golf in comfort:

Leave home in plenty of time.
Decide how many holes to play—and stick to it.
Take sufficient time for lunch and refuse to be rushed out afterwards.
Play foursomes whenever possible.

* * *

The District Council considered a proposal to erect a high fence, at ratepayers' expense, to prevent slices from the 18th tee of the local golf course.

With surprising unanimity the councillors voted down the idea—but their reasons followed closely their political affiliations.

'It would be wrong', declared the Labour leader, 'to use public money to subsidise the inaccuracies of well-to-do golfers'.

The Conservative chairman said they'd never had a fence there and why not leave things as they were.

And the sole Liberal councillor, although confessing to be a confirmed slicer, said it would infringe the freedom of the individual.

* * *

The ball out of bounds and those other abstract forms 'lost', 'unplayable' and 'provisional' are all associated with misfortune; and of the four 'provisional' deserves the most sympathy.

Like the mule, it has neither pride of ancestry nor hope of posterity. Introduced only in cases where the original ball may have encountered trouble, it is born of despair, is illegitimate from birth, and can gain an honest status only by being transformed into 'the ball in play'.

Since this change usually involves its owner in the loss of strokes the last state of the provisional ball is little better than the first.

* * *

Show me a man who can smile
When his drive goes into the ditch.
Show me a man who can laugh
When he's fluffed just a simple pitch.
Show me a man who can laugh
After missing the shortest of putts.
Show me this man. Find him if you can,
And I'll show you a guy who's NUTS.

* * *

Life's Little Problems:

What do you do when your opponent claims to have found his ball in the rough and you know he's a liar because his ball is in your pocket?

* * *

Some time ago in O'Connell Street, Dublin, I was gazing into the window of a well-known shoe shop (writes Mr Lee Williams of Torquay) which contained a selection of golf shoes lying on their sides to show their well-spiked soles.

A young Irishman at my side pointed to the spiked shoes and said to his companion: 'How in the name of God d'ye walk in those t'ings?'

* * *

Golf is a game in which the ball often lies badly but the golfer always lies well.

* * *

Arnold Palmer:

Golf is a game of inches the most important of which are those between the ears.

* * *

Mark Twain:

Golf is a good walk spoiled.

* * *

HE'S NOT THE BEST PLAYER IN THE CLUB—BUT HE NEVER LOSES A BALL IN THE ROUGH!

Players

This is not a book of cricket wit, so we can safely use the term 'Players' to cover amateurs of all kinds without fear of confusion. It may be observed in passing that not all Players of Golf are Gentlemen, for one meets all types, some of them objectionable, in the daily round. So our Players' Corner is as much a mixture as any other section. What all our characters have in common is an enthusiasm for the game—an enthusiasm which leads sometimes to gamesmanship or worse, but on the whole has beneficial and healthy effects on body, mind and soul.

Enthusiasm is not to be criticised, except by non-golfing individuals who perhaps have too much of it but must endure for the sake of harmony. Let the following be a warning to the new golfer bitten by the bug:

Before you move out on the first tee to test yourself, remember what you're letting yourself in for. Golf will take you over exactly like one of those body-snatching creatures in a space-fiction thriller. It will permeate all your waking moments and no doubt be the central theme of most of your dreams. You will be like the man whose wife berated him at breakfast with:

'All you ever think about is golf, golf, golf.'

'Aw, Sweetie', he protested. 'You know that's not so. Pass the putter, please.'

* * *

Dentist's receptionist (to irate patient in agony):

'I'm sorry, madam, but Mr Jenkins has been called out to a special case. Just fancy. He has to fill eighteen cavities, and said it would take him all morning.'

* * *

Two hard-hearted North Country men began what passes for a friendly game in that part of the world, and since the one hooked and the other sliced from the first tee, they did not meet again till they were on the green.

'How many?', asked Hobson. 'Seven', replied Winterbottom. 'Ah, then I've two for it', was the gruff response, as Hobson proceeded to putt up to the hole and knock in the next.

Again their paths diverged from the second tee and when once more together on the green Hobson began to speak. But the other held up his hand.

'My turn', he said, 'how many?'

* * *

Colonel Topmaster was a peppery old golfer who never spoke a word to anyone all the way round. One day he was drawn with a nervous young member in the club knock-out.

Hole after hole was played in complete silence until, as they walked off the 13th tee the young player ventured a conciliatory remark.

'That makes you two up, sir', he observed.

'Chatterbox,' snapped the Colonel.

* * *

Brown sliced his ball right across to the next fairway, nearly hitting a friend.

'Sorry about that, old boy', he called, 'but I did shout "*Fore*". Why didn't you duck? I might have killed you.'
'It wouldn't have mattered a damn', came the sorrowful reply. 'I took eleven at the last hole.'

* * *

The late Admiral Sir Charles Forbes of Wentworth, when Commander-in-Chief Home Fleet at Scapa Flow in World War II, was playing golf on Flotta Island when three shells landed in quick succession on a nearby fairway, sending the Admiral's fourball partners scrambling for cover.

The Admiral himself stood, driver in hand, with a gradually reddening face, until the firing ceased, and then resumed play, muttering: 'I'll have something to say to someone at the end of this round'.

And six miles away a young gunnery officer, who had miscalculated the range during a practice shoot of his cruiser's guns, was no doubt hoping that the C-in-C. would at least win his match.

* * *

An Aberdonian who claimed for a broken club was told by his insurance company that after 25 years of fair wear and tear it was of no value.

'Does that also apply to my life which has been insured with you for 35 years?' asked the golfer – and got the price of a new club.

* * *

A retired admiral walked towards the clubhouse steering and supporting a golfer who appeared to be in distress.

In response to concerned enquiries the old seadog shouted heartily: 'I was off course and shouted "*Fore*" but hit him aft'.

* * *

A bookmaker who was a keen golfer drove down a lane by a short hole and saw a boy hole his teeshot. As he got out of his car the boy teed up again – and once more holed in one.

The bookmaker met the boy as he came up to the green and said: 'Good gracious! How old are you?'

'Twelve', said the boy.

The bookmaker saw the chance of making money, persuaded the lad to accompany him to his home club, and there struck a match with the club champion at 10-1 against his new protégé.

But the lad took 10 at the first hole and went on in much the same way, losing heavily.

The bookmaker was furious. 'You've made me look a fool', he cried, 'pretending you couldn't play'.

'Don't be a fathead', replied the 12-year-old, 'you'll get 100-1 next week!'

* * *

Two visitors playing the second hole spotted the greenkeeper and one of them told him:

'When we were playing the first we saw a ball in the middle of the fairway. We were going to pick it up but decided to leave it.'

'Oh, I'm glad you did, sir', replied the greenkeeper. 'It belongs to old Colonel Bagginton-Fanshaw. He goes out every morning and has a couple of swipes at it, but misses each time, gets in a temper and goes back to the clubhouse.'

* * *

She was in love with him, had followed every shot of his tournament match, and had kissed him when he won.

He was infatuated with her, but also had the makings of a golf bore, and by the time he had talked for half-an-hour in the mixed lounge, going over his round, he sensed that her attention was wandering.

'But I'm talking all about myself, darling', he said. 'Now it's your turn. What did you think was the best shot I played this morning?'

* * *

A young man watching two players at a short hole saw one ball run a couple of yards past the hole and the other stop two feet short.

'That looks a pretty easy game', he said aloud.

'Do you play golf?' asked one of the players testily.

'No', was the answer.

'Then', said the player sharply, 'perhaps you'll just take this club and ball and see what you can do'.

The youngster stood up to the ball, held the club like a cricket bat, swung mightily, managed somehow to connect and watched while the ball raced on to the green, hit the flagstick with a big thump and dropped in.

'Thank goodness', he exclaimed, 'I thought for a moment that *I'd* missed as well'.

* * *

Geoffrey Roberts, winner of the 1951 English Amateur Championship, tells how he was sitting in the Hunstanton clubhouse after the first round of the final when a stranger said to him:

'Did you see that chap take three putts on the eighteenth green from ten feet. It was terrible. I could have done better myself.'

Then, seeing the competitor's badge in Roberts's lapel he added: 'I see you're a competitor. How far did you get?'

'I'm still in', answered Roberts. 'But I won't be much longer if I don't putt better than I did on the eighteenth.'

* * *

An English doctor in Bombay on a trip was called in to perform an emergency operation on a maharajah, and made a masterly job of it.

'You have saved my life', said the prince when he was convalescent, 'whatever you want shall be yours.'

'Oh, it was nothing, really', protested the surgeon.

'I insist', said His Highness.

'Well, I would go for a new matched set of golf clubs.'

'It is done.'

The surgeon returned to England and forgot about the matter until, six weeks later, he received this cable:

'Have your fourteen clubs but regret all not matched Stop Three are without swimming pools Stop.'

* * *

Jones sliced off the tee and his ball hit a man full tilt on the head, felling him to the ground.

Jones and his partner ran up to him, to find him sprawled out unconscious with the ball lying between his outstretched legs.

'Good heavens', cried Jones. 'What am I to do?'

'We ought not to move him', said the other player, 'so he becomes an immovable obstruction, and you can either play the ball as it lies or drop it two club-lengths away'.

* * *

Most handicap golfers have had the experience of 'going through' and then, by weak shots, holding up the players who had shown them courtesy. Mr Edge of Birmingham has a particular version of this embarrassment which did not include 'holding up', as his tale will show:

'I had not been playing golf very long, and on the local municipal course had played nine holes with three friends, when I had the honour on the tenth tee and went through the ritual mentally – 'check the grip, feet in line, ball not too high, target lined up . . . steady, watch that backswing . . . easy now . . .'

'Suddenly I had a feeling that something drastic was happening. I swung the club but it never reached the ball, because I was completely debagged. My trousers were down by my ankles, my partners were doubled up with laughter, likewise two elderly golfers approaching the ninth green, who had just given way to us. Very amusing to all except me . . .'

* * *

The first hole on the course was a short one, and the novice was being instructed in the game by a friend. Standing rather nervously he aimed a vicious swipe at the ball, which was half-topped, careered all the way to the green, hit the flagstick and dropped in.

'That's done it!' he cried, 'now I've lost my ball!'

* * *

'This', said the manager to the visiting VIP, 'is our latest computer which gives almost human reactions. Any question you like to ask will be answered immediately and correctly'.

'Where is my father?' asked the VIP. The wheels whirred, the lights flashed, and a sepulchral voice said: 'Your father has just driven off the first tee at St Andrews'.

'That's wrong for a start', said the VIP. 'My father's been dead ten years.'

'There must be some mistake', gasped the manager. He examined all the knobs and dials and said: 'Try again'.

'Where is my father who died ten years ago?' asked the visitor.

More whirrs and flashes and the voice spoke again:

'The man your mother married died ten years ago. Your father has just topped his second shot into the Swilken Burn.'

* * *

A golfer intrigued his fellow members when he was seen playing alone in a peculiar manner – alternately hitting a full shot, then kicking the ball forwards a few yards.

'What in the name of goodness are you doing?' a friend asked.

'Just practising – for the mixed foursomes on Sunday.'

* * *

Two golfers had been concerned for some time at the slow progress of two women, originally some holes ahead and now on the same fairway with every prospect of losing still more ground.

'I'll go on and ask if we can go through', said Brown, but had progressed only a few paces when he came back with a frown, saying:

'I say, old man, you'll have to do it. My wife is playing with my mistress.'

So Smith went forward, only to return even more swiftly.

'What a coincidence', he breathed.

* * *

The harassed-looking undersized golfer was wandering in the rough, club in hand, looking for his ball when two players overtook him.

'I suppose as a single player you'll let us through', asked one.

'I'm not single', replied the man with a sigh. 'I'm playing with my wife, but she's better than I am and has gone on ahead. I don't think you'll catch her.'

* * *

One player in a three-ball game walked into the clubhouse looking tired and worried and told the secretary that one of his partners had collapsed and died at the 9th hole, the farthest point on the course.

'How tragic', exlaimed the secretary. 'How can we get him back?'

'Oh, we've brought him back', said the player, 'we just couldn't leave him out there'.

'That must have been fearfully tiring for you both', observed the secretary.

'Well it was, but not the carrying. The trouble was putting him down and lifting him up between shots.'

* * *

Jenkins had lunched not wisely but too well and had only a hazy idea of things as he got under way in an afternoon foursome.

Just as he was about to putt on the first green a large black dog ran on and stood between his ball and the hole. He apparently took no notice and continued with his preparations to putt, when his partner exclaimed:

'I say, old man, let's get the dog away first.'

'Is that a real dog?' asked Jenkins, and welcomed the assurance with obvious relief.

* * *

In the days before roped-off fairways competitors often had to contend with scarcely manageable crowds, particularly on the famous Ayrshire links which were liable to be invaded by Lanarkshire miners, Clydeside shipworkers, and mechanics from industrial Irvine.

Hence the incident during a Championship at Troon when a harassed steward was trying to shepherd two competitors through a gallery massed around a green.

'Players, please', he called agitatedly.

'Tae hell wi' the players', was the retort from a burly miner. 'We've come to see'.

* * *

It may not be generally known that Dr W G Grace, whose autocratic ways at the crease are legendary, was a very keen golfer and at one time an honorary member of Walton Heath. Needless to say he could be just as intimidating with a golf club in his hand as with a bat. It is told of him that on his way to a golf match out of town he found himself at a station not on his direct route, and asked the booking clerk if his through ticket was available by that line.

The answer was in the negative whereupon the startled clerk was confronted by the head of a niblick thrust through the window and a mighty voice saying:

'Not available!'

Complete capitulation of the clerk.

* * *

'Reggie', said the Secretary as a member walked into the the club, 'there's a visitor out there wanting a game'.

'OK, I'll see what he's like. What's his handicap?'

'Twelve.'

Three hours later the pair returned and after a couple of drinks the visitor left.

'How did you get on?' asked the Secretary.

'A fine old-fashioned twelve if ever I saw one', exploded Reggie. 'He never missed a drive, played every iron shot as though he knew the course inside out, and one-putted six greens!'

'Good gracious! What was he round in?'

'Seventy-two. Six under par with his handicap.'

'And what did he win by?'

'Win? I beat him 4 and 3!'

* * *

A visitor was about to play with the Club captain and members waiting their turn stood back to give this pair the courtesy of the tee. The visitor had a couple of practice swings, then prepared to drive. Giving a mighty lunge he missed the ball completely, and then proceeded to have three more air shots.

There was a pained silence, broken by the visitor who, with a sheepish grin, said:

'I'm sorry, gentlemen. The trouble is my course is three inches higher than this one.'

* * *

Four golfers were playing their usual Saturday fourball when along an adjacent road came a funeral procession. One of them stood reverently, cap in hand, until the cortège was out of sight.

'Someone you know?' enquired one of the other players, sympathetically.

'Someone I know!' he exclaimed, 'We'd been married 27 years!'

* * *

Tense situation on the last green in the 36 holes final. Players all square, one ball seven yards from the pin, the other five yards. Green undulating and full of hidden borrows.

Player No 1 has a quick look at the line, steps up and strikes the ball sweetly, straight into the hole for a birdie three.

Player No 2 has a look at his line, walks to the other end for a second look, then surveys the situation from the side. Finally he calls his caddie to have a look.

Spectators fidget as player and caddie have a long consultation. The minutes go by. Player crouches down for another long look, then straightens up, picks up his ball and walks with outstretched hand towards his opponent.

'Impossible!' he mutters, and, shaking hands, turns slowly away.

* * *

'Anything wrong?' asked the passenger as a bumping noise began at the rear of the car and the driver immediately swung into a nearby garage.

'No, I just want petrol', he answered. He filled up and drove off, whereupon the passenger observed that the bumping had stopped.

'Yes, that's my petrol gauge,' laughed the driver, 'My small boy dropped a golf ball into the tank, and when it starts rolling I know I'm wanting petrol.'

* * *

Some young bloods in the clubhouse bar had an argument about drinking and one was challenged to drink six pints of beer inside three minutes.

'Just a moment', he said, and hurried from the bar, leaving his friends to conjecture whether he was dodging the issue or merely clearing decks for action. A few minutes later he returned, accepted the challenge, and when the six foaming tankards were lined up drained them all inside the limit.

'Where did you go before you started?' asked one of the losers.

'Into the mixed bar to make sure I could do it.'

* * *

Humphrey Ellis, although an England international, was a golfer of the traditional school and had no time at all for statistics or evaluations of performance. On one occasion at Rye he had played so well that his admiring caddie, when his master was about to play a chip shot just short of the home green, observed that if he got down in two strokes he would beat the course record.

'Is that so, caddie?' was the calm response. 'Then give me my brassie.' With the clubs exchanged he faced about and swiped the ball back towards the tee.

* * *

An American visiting Britain was determined to play at one of the most exclusive clubs in the Home Counties – a club with a membership list looking like pages from Debrett, and full of traditional conservatism.

After some trouble he obtained a letter of introduction and set off from the Savoy, conjuring up dreams of a magnificent opulent set-up at least equivalent to the most exclusive American country club. Instead he drove up to a modest red-brick building with an oak nail-studded door which was closed. He rang the bell and a dignified-looking figure, looking like a butler, but announcing himself as the steward, took his letter of introduction.

'The Secretary, sir, is away', he said, 'but with a letter of introduction you may play. Unfortunately there is no member here at the moment, we have no caddies – and, as you see, it is raining hard.'

But our American was not to be put off. Out he went, shouldering his bag, played all the way round and returned tired and soaked to the skin.

'Where's the drying room?' he asked.

'There is no drying-room, sir.'

'Hell, then I'll just have a shower.'

'We've no showers, sir.'

'Hell, What do the members do when they get wet?'

'Their lordships, sir, always go home to change.'

* * *

How the Other Half Live

A wealthy American tourist arrived at a small Irish hotel and walked to the tiny reception window while through the doors came not only his suitcases but also golf clubs, golf shoes, golf umbrella, and several boxes of balls.

'There must be some mistake, sir', cried the manager, distracted by the interruption. 'There's no golf course within miles of this hotel.'

'No problem,' drawled the visitor. 'I'm having that sent over with my heavy baggage.'

* * *

Two golfers were walking off the last green when one of them collapsed. The unfortunate man was taken to the hospital in the ambulance and his partner went with him, waiting for news of his condition.

Eventually a doctor came out to tell him his friend was showing signs of recovery.

'Good', was the reply. 'When he's fully conscious will you remind him he owes me five shillings on today's game, and that I'll be waiting on the first tee next Sunday as usual.'

* * *

'Andy' said Jock, accosting his old friend, 'can ye see your way to letting me have a golf ball?'

'I thought you'd stopped playing golf', said Andy, reluctantly extracting a ball from his bag.

'Well, I'm doing it by degrees', replied Jock, pocketing the ball. 'In the first place, I've stopped buying balls.'

* * *

Percy Huggins, Editor of 'Golf Monthly' and a colleague of many years' standing, has contributed to this anthology several good Scottish stories but one we particularly like, mainly because we know the character concerned, tells of 'Hammy' (otherwise Hamilton) McInally, three times Scottish Amateur Champion.

In an early round of the 1946 Amateur Championship at Royal Birkdale he was playing a distinguished English player and driving, as he sometimes did, with a No 1 iron.

After a few holes his opponent commented: 'I see you're not using your woods today. Are you having trouble with them?'

'Oh, no,' replied Hammy, 'I'll be using them the morrer'. and he was.

* * *

He's what I call a mathematical golfer. He shouts 'fore', takes six, and puts down five.

* * *

A man walking across the course was hit on the leg by a golf ball and shook his fist at the apologetic player.

'I claim damages', he shouted.

'But didn't you hear me call "fore"?' asked the player.

'No I didn't, but I won't settle for anything less than a fiver.'

* * *

THAT WAS HOW I PLAYED THE FIRST HOLE, NOW WHEN I TEED OFF FOR THE SECOND . . .

Heard on the Course

A golfer at St Andrews set off cheerfully on a sunny morning and gaily hit a mashie shot to the green. As his ball sailed safely over the Swilken Burn he cried:

'That's right, my bonny. Over the wee bonny brook wi'ye.'

In the afternoon, with a similar shot to play, he topped his ball. As it raced towards a watery grave he raised his club and yelled: 'Och, ye daftie. Into the stinking ditch, is it?'

* * *

'Is my good friend in the bunker – or has the bastard skipped it?'

* * *

Woman spectator, more accustomed to the stars of show-business than to those of the links, was told that one of a group of professionals was Max Faulkner.

'Oh', she breathed, 'how exciting. I've always wanted to meet Max Factor in the flesh'.

* * *

Child (after watching a golfer make several fruitless attempts to get out of a bunker):

'It must be dead by now, Mummy. He's stopped hitting it.'

* * *

'Did you hear about old George collapsing at the seventh hole.'

'Yes. Harold gave him the kiss of life and was drunk for seven hours.'

* * *

'I didn't think he had a brassie lie in that rough.'

'He didn't – until he started addressing the ball.'

* * *

A retired naval officer noted for his language was drawn against a member who disliked swearing. The Secretary implored the former to smother his feelings, and he did so for several holes.

But a shanked iron shot at the sixth was too much for him and a four-letter word reverberated over the course. Whereupon he walked across the fairway to his opponent and said:

'I do beg your pardon. I meant to say bugger.'

* * *

'Your trouble is that you're not addressing the ball correctly.'

'Well you must admit I was polite to the darned thing for a long time.'

* * *

'Have you quarrelled with Johnson? You don't play together any more.'

'Would you go on playing with a fellow who kicks your ball into a worse lie or moves his own into a better one when you're not looking?'

'Of course not.'

'Well, neither will Johnson.'

* * *

'Hallo – new set of clubs, old man?'

'Yes, I've just got them for the wife.'

'Well, I hope you'll be satisfied with the bargain.'

* * *

'How are your lessons going on?'

'No good at all. I did exactly as I was told – kept my head down and my eye on the ball. And someone stole my golf bag.'

* * *

In the days when a ball obstructing another on the green created a stymie (now eliminated by rule) a young man and his girl friend played blind shots to a bowl-shaped green. The man reached the ridge first, looked down at the green and called:

'It's a stymie – a dead stymie.'

'I thought I could smell something dreadful', she replied, wrinkling her pretty nose.

* * *

'Giving up golf, Jock! Why, have you lost interest?'
'Na, na. Lost ma ball.'

* * *

'That can't be my ball, caddie. It looks far too old?'
'It's a long time since we started, sir.'

* * *

Professionals

The great days of humour among professional golfers are past – for several reasons. The old-time pro was a very human individual, occupying a very special niche in a golfing community, in which he achieved a personality. His utterances, whether words of wise advice, pawky comments on his contemporaries, or keen ripostes in argument, were quoted within a small circle of cronies, supporters and patrons. When he played in a big match he had a close attendance of spectators who could hear what he said to his opponent, his exchanges with his caddie, and his asides to onlookers.

Nowadays circumstances are very different. The great majority of professionals are educated men accustomed to dealing with customers on an equal footing. Those who concentrate on their members and shops have a businesslike approach to their affairs; those who play on the tournament circuit can allow no distraction to affect their efforts to win the big prizes. In both cases there is little room for humour. And in the case of the tournament professionals, they are now so segregated from the spectators that any quotable remarks would fall on so few ears as to have little hope of getting into general circulation.

Nevertheless, in our selection of stories by or about professionals we have included some modern ones in addition to those having the true flavour of the old days – the days of Andra' Kirkaldy, for instance.

Andra' Kirkaldy fought at the Battle of Omdurman but later gave up soldiering to settle at St Andrews, where he rapidly became renowned for his caustic wit and adventures with frail femininity.

He was appointed professional to the Royal and Ancient Golf Club and until his death in 1934 was accustomed to sit on a kitchen chair at the back of the Tom Morris green on any big occasion, rising to hold the flagstick while each successive couple putted. Such a procedure would now be contrary to rule, but we wonder whether anyone, even the Secretary of the R and A, would have had the temerity to remonstrate with Andra'.

There is one story of a brush with authority, when Andra' was due to go before the Committee to answer for some misdemeanour. An elderly member of the Club urged him to be subservient and keep his temper.

'After all', observed the wise counsellor, 'you might lose your job and then ye might starve, Andra'.'

'What!' cried Andra'. 'Me starve – and friends with half the cooks in St. Andrews!'

* * *

Andra' often had matches with Wee Ben Sayers of North Berwick, and on one of these occasions, which induced great partisanship, Wee Ben sliced his drive into a deep bunker. The little man disappeared into the hazard while Andra' waited on the other side of the fairway for his turn to play.

Some minutes elapsed and eventually a supporter went up to Andra' and said suspiciously:

'Wee Ben is a long time in that bunker, Andra' '. 'A-weel', replied Kirkaldy. 'I have nae doot he's making guid use o' his time.'

* * *

On another occasion Sayers and Kirkaldy were playing at St Andrews when Kirkaldy put his ball on to the railway which in those days was not out of bounds.

Andra', surveying his ball lying in the rubble on which the sleepers were laid, called: 'Lend me your wee mashie, Ben.'

'Na, na', replied Sayers, 'break your ain damned club.'

* * *

Professional (to player just in from the course):

'Mr. Jones, did you hook off the fifth tee over the hedge?'

'That's right, Smith. I never troubled to look for it.'

'That's a pity, because the ball landed on the road just in front of a pony-and-trap. The pony bolted and ran the trap into a car which went off the road into the hedge. Three people were taken to hospital and the pony had to be destroyed.

'Good heavens! What on earth shall I do?'

'What I'm always telling you to do, Mr Jones. Hold the right hand more on top of the shaft.'

* * *

'I've just seen Mr Simpson dashing off to the practice ground', said the assistant to the pro.

'Yes, I've sold him a new driver.'

'That won't do him any more good than the last one you sold him.'

'Perhaps not. But for the moment he's happy.'

* * *

During a tour of the United States early in his career George Duncan, the 1920 Open Champion, played an exhibition match in the Deep South, his clubs carried by a big negro.

In those days (in Britain at any rate) the golfer was accustomed to tapping with the head of his driver on the spot where he wished the caddie to build a tee of sand. On this occasion Duncan went through the ritual on the first tee and his caddie just looked, uncomprehending. Duncan tapped again, somewhat impatiently and said:

'I want the ball teed there, caddie.'

The negro's eyes rolled in sympathy.

'What's the matter, sah? You got lumbago?'

* * *

A golfer asked his professional, a veteran of 72, for a lesson.

'I can manage tomorrow morning', was the reply, 'but in the afternoon I must go to visit my father.'

'Your father', said the golfer incredulously, 'how old is he?'

'He's 95.'

'And does he play golf, too?'

'Well, he knocks the ball about a bit – but he'll never make a player.'

* * *

Seen in a London professional's shop:

An old marble clock with the works removed and in their place a notice saying: 'Sorry, no tick.'

* * *

Bobby Locke, four times Open Champion, was playing with the most conceited golfer ever born. But he admired Bobby, and asked advice quite often. At the tenth he topped his drive all along the ground, but the ball struck a rock and ricocheted into the branches of a tree, where it was held several feet up.

'How would you play that?' asked the amateur.

'Under an assumed name', replied Bobby.

* * *

In an upstairs room in a St Andrews house the old champion lay ill. Several of his friends, up for the Championship, came in a body to see him, but before they went up the leader called for a whip-round. Then they walked in, assembled round the bed, and talked in whispers while the invalid surveyed them through lack-lustre eyes and said not a word.

Finally the leader pressed twenty pound-notes into one of the hands lying inert on the pillow and gave the signal to depart. They were passing through the door when a call of 'Hi, you fellows!' from the bed stopped them in their tracks.

There was the invalid, bolt upright; his eyes shining and his face wreathed in smiles. Waving the notes clutched tightly in his hand he cried: 'Glad to see you, boys. Come again whenever you like.'

* * *

Harry Vardon was once asked by a woman to join the temperance movement.

'Madam', he replied, 'moderation is essential in all things, but I have never failed to beat a teetotaller.'

* * *

Exchange of Pleasantries Department:

One of the toughest games in the 1957 Ryder Cup match, which Britain won, was between Eric Brown and Tommy Bolt of the United States, noted for his bad temper.

Brown won on the 33rd green at Lindrick and Bolt, shaking hands, said grumpily:

'Well, Eric, you beat me, but I didn't enjoy the game one little bit.'

'Tommy, said Brown, 'you didn't have a chance.'

In the clubhouse an Englishman of the old school said: 'Jolly bad luck, Bolt. You put up a damned good show. I'm sorry you lost.'

Tommy took off his cap and threw it down in anger, shouting: 'The hell with that. You're glad!'

* * *

Walter Hagen, notable for his late nights and ability to strike winning form on the morning after, wandered back to his hotel well after midnight. A well-intentioned friend observed that Hagen ought to make more careful preparation for that day's match with Leo Diegel, and remarked that Diegel had been in bed some hours.

'Yeah', drawled Hagen, 'but is he sleeping?'

* * *

'I don't want to be a millionaire', Hagen once observed, 'I only want to live like one.'

* * *

'How's your daughter's golf?' asked the professional.

'Pretty good', said the proud father, 'she's going round in less and less every time she plays.'

'H'm', pondered the professional, 'I'd better have a look at her.'

* * *

Bobby Locke as a rule talks to no-one outside his match and never seems to notice anyone on the course. But there are exceptions, as this story from his book (Bobby Locke on Golf, Country Life) *indicates:*

'There were two Americans following me closely and I could not help overhearing their conversation. One of them said: 'Gee, this old guy from Africa is really turning on the heat.' A lot of Americans found it difficult to believe my age, insisting that I was at least 40. I could not resist turning round and asking 'How old do you think I am, anyway?' One of them replied: 'About 43.' I laughed and said: 'No, sir, you're twelve years out.' With a broad smile he came again and said: 'What! 55?'

* * *

In another story Locke relates:

'I totted up my winnings for the season (1947 in the United States). I had pocketed 27,500 dollars, coming second to Jimmy Demaret. Someone remarked in my hearing: Locke's trouble is his left hand is weak. 'Don't worry about that', I retorted, 'I take the cheques with my right hand.'

* * *

A rather pompous amateur was playing against a professional, and on one green, looking at his ball a foot from the hole, said to his opponent:

'You don't want me to hole that!'

'No', said the professional, and the amateur, picking up the ball, walked to the next tee and proceeded to take the honour.

'My honour, I think', said the professional, 'I won the last hole, as you didn't putt out.'

'But you said you didn't want me to hole out', blustered the amateur.

'That's right. I didn't. And you didn't.'

* * *

A famous professional hit his drive far into the woods, and not for the first time in the round.

Turning to his caddie he said:

'Give me my axe.'

* * *

'I believe you make more money in a year than Harold Wilson does', observed an inquisitive stranger to a leading tournament pro.

'I suppose I do', was the cool reply, 'and why not? I'm a better golfer than he is.'

* * *

The late Archie Compston had a ruthless attitude to most things – including golf balls – and was not always careful about his choice of language. On one occasion a golf partner played a trick on Archie by putting the great man's putter into his own bag.

They reached the first green. Archie looked for his putter and abused his caddie for leaving it behind.

Then the partner produced the missing club, only to receive abuse in his turn.

'You can take a man's wife' thundered Archie. 'You can even take his wallet. But never on any account take a man's putter.'

* * *

Andra Kirkaldy stories pop up from time to time. Here's one about a visit he and a few cronies paid to a high-class restaurant when they were in funds.

They enjoyed the meal but were stunned when the bill was handed to Andra' and he showed it around. Then he groped in his pocket, counted out the exact sum required and handed it to the expectant waiter.

The man looked at the notes and coins in his tray and said:

'You'll no' be forgetting the waiter, sir?'

'Nae', retorted Andra', 'I'll no' be forgetting him, and I'll no' forgie him either.'

* * *

Ronald Heager, Golf Correspondent of The Daily Express (London) *and Hon Secretary of the British Association of Golf Writers, remembers one of the flashes of Arnold Palmer humour which perhaps consoled British ex-amateur Guy Wolstenholme for an accident.*

Wolstenholme began a tour of the US winter circuit in 1962, but this was cut short after three weeks when he played a final practice round at Cypress Point for the Bing Crosby tournament. Wolstenholme for some reason jumped on to what appeared to be a tree-stump. But it was a loose log and Wolstenholme was sent crashing to the ground, breaking his arm.

The actual hole where this occurred was the famous sixth, where the teeshot is across water to a peninsula green – one of the toughest holes in golf.

After the accident a sad Wolstenholme encountered Palmer who consoled with him and asked where it happened. He was told.

'I always knew it was one helluva hole', remarked Arnie, 'but I didn't realise it's so tough it can break your arm.'

* * *

Jack Nicklaus doesn't relax so easily as Arnie but he can come up with the bright answer now and again. Ron Heager, who no doubt would concede that The Golden Bear has a laconic wit, recalls a fellow-journalist saying to Nicklaus in the R and A clubhouse during the 1964 Open:

'I see, Jack, you've discovered the secret of the Old Course.'

'Yeah', drawled Jack, 'fewer putts.'

* * *

NOT ONLY IS HE WILD OFF THE TEE—HE'S
EVEN BEEN KNOWN TO SHOUT 'FORE'
ON THE GREEN!

There's No Golf Like Show-biz Golf

Whenever we meet a member of the Vaudeville Golfing Society or, indeed, any other golfer in show-business, we expect to be up against an opponent in full practice. Weekday mornings see many stars of stage, screen, TV and radio in action on golf courses all over the country. The VGS has a working arrangement with many golf clubs, and what greater relaxation from the routine of rehearsals and performances can be imagined than two or three hours in the fresh air trying to play to one's handicap?

Many of our friends of the entertainment world are extremely good golfers, but even the lesser lights (in a golfing sense) have their contributions to make to our little collection of humorous stories. Some of them really do have hilarious moments, but all, without exception, are adept at adorning the tale, if not pointing the moral. So for the following selection of stories by or about the show-biz people we take no responsibility whatever.

Not even for the one by Bob Monkhouse of the man who went to bed with his golf clubs.

His wife remonstrated (unreasonable woman!) whereupon he retorted: 'You said I had to choose between you and my golf clubs.'

* * *

Comedians Harry Secombe and Eric Sykes were both in the same bunker and all that could be seen of their operations were flurries of sand. After this had been going on for some time Harry was heard to say to Eric:

'Don't you think we'd better stop this lark and sing *The Desert Song.*'

* * *

Bob Hope: 'Hey, Jack, what impresses you most about my golf.'

Jack Nicklaus: 'Your score-keeping.'

* * *

More 'Hope-Full' Remarks:

My old friend Jack Benny has had only one golf ball all his life. And now he's lost it. The string came off.

* * *

Old Man Crosby and I play a lot of golf together and often play for sidestakes. The only trouble is that when I win I have to engage an attorney to get my money.

* * *

Not everyone knows that when Bing goes out to play he takes thirteen clubs and a stomach pump. And after every bad shot he takes poison.

* * *

Now its Bing's Turn:

Bob Hope rags Bing Crosby about his age and his golf, but Bing has been known to get his own back. Art Buchwald, American columnist, tells of how he chatted with Crosby during a round at St Cloud, the singer's clubs being carried by a woman caddie.

Bing played haphazardly, obviously not concentrating, and at the end the woman caddie said:

'You'd do better if you didn't talk to him' (indicating Buchwald).

'Now if I were Hope', commented Bing, 'I'd send for a writer and have an answer to that.'

* * *

From Joe (Mr Piano) Henderson:

An old tramp wandered on to the golf course, walked leisurely up the eighteenth fairway to the green. There he sat down, and from an old sack took a handful of dried twigs and two pieces of iron rod, which he fixed to form an arch over the twigs. Then he suspended from the rods a can of water, and lit the fire.

He sat musing on the thought of a nice 'cuppa' when a man ran from the clubhouse and in no uncertain language ordered him off.

'Who do you think you are?' asked the tramp.

'I'm the Secretary of the Club', boomed the other.

'Well let me give you a piece of advice, Mr Secretary', said the tramp. 'That's not the right way to get new members.'

* * *

Comedian David Nixon told this one at a golf dinner.

A golfer came into the clubhouse looking anything but pleased. 'I've just been playing with a chap who is a Civil Servant', he explained. Playing the 17th someone shouted 'fore' and he sat down to wait for a cup of tea. I've come in and left him sitting there.'

* * *

Two Rays of Sunshine

The game of golf has given us two Ted Rays, one a professional player and the other a professional comedian, but each in his own way a natural humourist.

Ted Ray the Guernsey Islander, with his big pipe, his shapeless felt hat, and his vigorous sway, won the Open Championship in 1912 and the United States Open in 1920, and was known on both sides of the Atlantic for his down-to-earth comments.

Once he was approached by an admirer of his big hitting who said:

'Mr Ray, can you tell me how I can drive farther than I do?'

Ted took his pipe from his mouth, regarded his questioner solemnly, and then said:

'Hit it a bloody sight 'arder, mate.'

* * *

Ted Ray the comedian may not be in the championship class as a golfer, but his fund of good stories is inexhaustible.

'I found a new golf ball on the fairway just after playing a shot', he said once. 'Then, after playing my next shot, I found another. And then another. And then I found a hole in the ball-pocket of my bag.'

* * *

Ted's special contribution to our collection is this gem:

A very indifferent golfer (but one with a sense of humour) walked into a sports' outfitter's shop and said to the salesman:

'Have you any of these new atomic golf balls which give out signals in the rough to let you know where they are?'

Without batting an eyelid the salesman replied 'Yes, sir, you can get them at the Geiger Counter.'

* * *

HE'S BEEN KNOWN TO PLAY FROM MORNING TILL NIGHT WITHOUT PLAYING THE SAME HOLE TWICE

Women Golfers

In the sixty years or so since women golfers were emancipated from the handicaps of straw-hats, wasp waists and ankle-length skirts lined with petticoats, the game on the distaff side has progressed beyond belief. So much so that anyone watching a tournament for women in these days will scarcely credit the fact that when the first British Ladies' Championship was planned in 1893, shortly after the formation of the Ladies' Golf Union, most men gave the idea short shrift.

One of the LGU officials asked a well-known golfer what he thought about it, and in a letter he expressed himself extremely sceptical for the following reasons:

Women never have and never can unite to push any scheme to success. They are bound to fall out and quarrel on the slightest provocation.

They will never go through one Championship with credit.

Constitutionally and physically women are unfitted for golf. They will never last through two rounds of a long course in a day. Nor can they ever hope to defy the wind and weather. Temperamentally the strain will be too much for them. The first Ladies' Championship will be the last, unless I and others are greatly mistaken.

Just 30 years later the late Miss Mabel E Stringer (Auntie Mabel) was able to quote this with amusement in her *Golfing Reminiscences*, published by Mills & Boon, London, in 1924.

But the real progress towards complete freedom has been made over the last 30 years. Women golfers of today are as free as their Victorian predecessors were restricted. The mixed bar is now the main one in most clubhouses, locker accommodation for women members is often superior to that for the men; and little by little equality of the sexes is being approached in such matters as playing hours. Naturally, therefore our *Ladies' Section* will contain a mixture of old and new, beginning with some words written by a certain Lord Wellwood in 1890 which only amuse us today but were endorsed by every male golfer in the country at the time they were written:

'*We venture to suggest 70 or 80 yards as the average limit of a drive*', *wrote his lordship*, '*not because we doubt a lady's power to make a longer drive, but because that cannot well be done without raising the club above the shoulder. Now we do not presume to dictate, but we must observe that the posture and gestures requisite for a full swing are not particularly graceful when the player is clad in female dress.*'

* * *

A golfer marvelling at the enormous distances achieved by Mildred Didrikson Zaharias (The Babe) asked her how she accomplished such tremendous feats:

'I just loosen my girdle and let fly' was the succinct response.

* * *

'The difference between Babe Zaharias and myself', said Bob Hope, 'is that I hit the ball like a girl and she hits it like a man.'

* * *

The pretty young girl, long in handicap and short in experience, was drawn to partner the club champion in the mixed foursomes and received some stern advice at the start:

'Just keep the ball in play and leave the rest to me', he said, and a few moments later hit a cannon-ball drive nearly 300 yards down the fairway.

She made a brave effort with her iron shot and succeeded in moving the ball three or four yards.

He breathed heavily, produced a five-iron and walloped the ball on to the green, two feet from the hole.

Somehow she managed to miss the putt and he looked very grim as he tapped it in for a five.

'We'll have to do better than that', he observed on their way to the next tee, 'five shots for a drive-and-pitch hole!'

'Well don't forget', was the demure reply, 'that you took three of them.'

* * *

'You think so much of your golf you don't even remember when we were married.'

'Oh, yes I do, dear. It was the day I beat old Jones 9 and 7.'

* * *

The scene is reputed to have been Leslie King's golf school in the West End of London when two ladies called to make an appointment for a lesson.

'Do you both wish lessons?' asked the receptionist.

'No,' said one lady. 'It's my friend. I learnt last week.'

* * *

'Cynthia played beautifully until she broke a shoulder strap.'

* * *

At one of the early meetings of the Ladies' Golf Union half-an-hour or more was spent trying to word a resolution to everyone's satisfaction. Miss Blanche Hulton, the Hon Treasurer, could stand it no longer.

'This is only a resolution', she said, 'not a sixpenny telegram.' Laughter – and a speedy end to the discussion.

* * *

When Babe Zaharias arrived at Gullane, Scotland, to play in the British championship, which she won, she was allotted a caddie who looked to be about 80. The story goes that when she asked the caddie-master if she couldn't have a younger caddie, he produced a man who said he was 75.

* * *

After the British women's team had beaten America in the Curtis Cup match at Muirfield in 1952 the Captain, the late Lady Katharine Cairns, sent a telegram to the LGU President reading:

'We have done our damndest.' Back came the reply: 'Deplore your language but glory in your victory.'

* * *

Two Irish girls on a course near Dublin:

Kate: 'Look there, Bridget, the Archbishop playing with his dog and throwing sticks for it.'

Bridget: 'Indeed I see him. Just like the big boy he is, bless him.'

Kate (after a closer look): 'But I'm wrong, Bridget – it's the Protestant one.'

Bridget: 'Och, the old fule that he is.'

* * *

'So the Judge fined you fifty dollars for hitting your wife.'

'Well, it wasn't so much for hitting her as for using the wrong club.'

* * *

There's no knowing what the statistical hounds and pollsters will get up to next. In America they analysed the usual 'average sample' to find out why women take up golf and came up with the following answers:

47 per cent to skip housework.
25 per cent to find a husband.
17 per cent to play bridge.
8 per cent to keep tabs on their husbands.
3 per cent because they like the game.

* * *

Sixty years ago Mitcham, Surrey, was a favourite resort of aristocratic golfers, wealthy golfers, Members of Parliament, – and women players. Hence the following limerick (circa 1900):

There was a young golfer of Mitcham
Who tried, when approaching, to pitch 'em.
But she played with a chop,
Hit her ball on the top,
And the only result was to ditch 'em.

* * *

During the morning round in the British Ladies' Championship final at St Andrews in 1929 Glenna Collett, the famous American player, was five up on Joyce Wethered, who subsequently won the match.

A stranger whose only purpose in visiting St Andrews was to explore the Cathedral ruins and University Buildings was surprised and mystified to be addressed by a postman doing his rounds, who muttered gloomily:

'She's five doon.' The stranger no doubt went on his way pondering the strange habits of these St Andreans.

* * *

Major John Bywaters, Secretary of the Professional Golfers' Association, includes among his many good after-dinner stories the tale of his embarrassing first day as a golf club secretary.

Having finished my morning in the office I went into the lounge and saw, leaning against the bar, a tall individual with a weather-beaten face wearing brown corduroy trousers and enjoying a pint of bitter.

Anxious to make a good impression I said: 'Good morning, sir. It's a lovely day.'

It was the Lady Captain.

* * *

An unpopular woman member who was the subject of considerable gossip came flaming into the secretary's office just before lunch and cried:

'Mrs Jones has insulted me and I demand an apology and her resignation.'

'What's happened now?', asked the weary secretary, fed up with the frequent quarrels.

'We were playing the last hole all square in our tournament match when Mrs Jones came over and accused me of moving my ball in the rough.

'I said 'You're a liar' and she said 'I'd sooner be a liar than what you are – or rather, at your age, what you've been.' What do you think of that?'

'Ah, well, my dear lady, really it's nothing to get worried about', replied the Secretary. 'After all, I've been out of the Army sixteen years but they still call me Colonel.'

* * *

One of our Danish friends, Mr F Kinck Petersen, tells us that after a round at Copenhagen Golf Club he repaired with his opponent to the 19th hole where another member was consoling himself with a strong drink.

He gave a sad smile in response to their greetings and said:

'It is hopeless.'

'What is wrong?' he was asked.

'I have come the conclusion', he replied with a sigh, 'that my relationship to golf is the same as my relationship to my wife – I love her but I cannot control her.'

* * *

There was no more popular personality in golf than the late Jack Buckley-Lowe, who was Secretary of the Old Links Club at St Annes, Lancashire, for more than 50 years. He told us once that he received the following letter from a lady member:

'Dear Sir, Since I visited you in your office yesterday I have decided to tender my resignation from the club. I find that I am no longer able to engage in active sports.'

* * *

It was in the early days of Press coverage of golf tournaments and the Secretary of a West of England club, already turned upside down by the influx of competitors and officials for a National women's championship, was taken aback when two journalists from London asked for permission to use the lounge as a writing room.

'I suppose it will be all right', he said doubtfully, 'so long as you don't interfere with the competitors.'

* * *

This is – believe us – the truest of all the true stories in this book.

At a Surrey golf club two ladies were playing when a madman rushed out of the bushes clad in nothing at all.

'Sir', asked the older of the two players severely, leaning on her club, 'are you a member?'

* * *

HE'S A GOLFING POLITICIAN—HE PROMISES A LOT AND DOES NOTHING

Saints and Sinners

It has been said that on Mondays, when clerical golfers disport themselves on the links, the silence is more profane than the customary noise of other days.

* * *

An old Scots professional used to tell of the man of the cloth, well-known for his advocacy of golf as a test of self-control, who in a moment of exasperation flung his club away. Seeing the professional watching him he said sadly:

'Well, Sandy, I'm better at preaching than practising. I feel like breaking my clubs over my knee.'

'Try swearing', urged Sandy, 'it's a grand thing for letting off steam.'

* * *

A vicar playing his regular weekly game with an elder of his flock suffered his customary defeat. Seeing that the loser was looking a trifle more depressed than usual, the winner observed on the way to the clubhouse:

'Cheer up, vicar. You'll be burying me eventually.'

'Even then,' was the inconsolable reply, 'it'll be your hole.'

* * *

St Peter and St John were playing golf on the celestial links and they halved the first seventeen holes, in birdie figures, of course. They came to the last hole – a short one – and St John's ball, played too strong, seemed certain to go over the green.

But it struck the flag and dropped from its folds down the stick and into the hole.

'You've that for the half', said St John as St Peter teed up in turn, 'and none of your blooming miracles.'

* * *

A parson at St Andrews, seeing a good drive fade into a bunker, stifled an unbecoming expression and instead muttered:

'Vade retro, Satanus.'

'Nane o' that foreign swearing here', said the caddie, 'Remember, ye're in Scotland.'

* * *

An Irish priest on holiday in South Africa sliced his teeshot into truly jungle country and after some search found his ball – guarded by a huge lion. Falling to his knees the priest began to pray and to his amazement the lion followed suit.

'Heaven be praised', exclaimed the priest, 'a practising Christian lion.'

'Quiet,' roared the lion, 'while I'm saying grace.'

* * *

St Thomas and St Peter were playing golf one heavenly afternoon and St Peter holed out in one at the 346 yards first hole. Then St Thomas had a go and also holed in one.

'That's a half,' said St Peter, 'and now let's cut out the miracles and have a golf match.'

* * *

The three non-clericals playing with a clergyman preserved a virtuous control over their remarks until one of them shanked into a pond and could not repress a good honest oath.

He apologised immediately to the clergyman and added:

'But there must be times when you get annoyed with a shot. How do you let off steam?'

'My friend', replied the clergyman, 'all I do is say the names of some of my congregation – with emphasis.'

*　*　*

Many clergymen in Scotland, in the early days of the game, were just as devoted to golf as their parishioners, but inhibited by their cloth from giving the same vent to their feelings. One unfortunate incumbent, suffering even worse form than usual, at length uttered an expression most unsuited to his calling and was properly rebuked by his partner, another minister.

'It's nae guid', he replied, 'I'll juist hae to gie it up.'

'What', said his horrified companion, 'gie up gowf?'

'Nae, nae', was the reply, 'gie up the kirk.'

*　*　*

The golfer was transported to Heaven and found it was a magnificent golf course flanked by trees, like a celestial Pinehurst. With his angel guide he set out to explore and the first player he saw was shaping to cut the corner of a dogleg, a feat demanding a carry of at least 300 yards.

'That shot will be a miracle', observed, the newcomer, 'who does he think he is – St Peter?'

'It happens to *be* St Peter', whispered the angel, 'but he thinks he's Arnold Palmer.'

*　*　*

The keen golfer had led a dissolute life and was not surprised to find himself in hell, but very relieved to see that his abode was a palatial golf club with bubbling brooks, a serene lake, beautifully cut fairways, putting greens like billiard tables, and a professional's shop bearing the notice:

'All equipment free – help yourself.'

Very excited, he grabbed a bag full of golf clubs and a handful of teepegs, rushed to the first tee, took out a driver and swung it with glee. Then he bent to the ball pocket only to discover it empty. He turned on his heels to return to the shop but a man dressed in plus fours and sitting dejectedly on a seat held up his hand.

'No good trying to get golf balls', he said. 'There aren't any. That's the hell of it.'

* * *

The young curate had always managed to indulge in his passion for golf within the bounds of his religious duty. But a transfer to a church right alongside a golf course proved too big a trial. One Sunday in high summer he rose at dawn to prepare for the day's ceremonies but could not resist the temptation to play a hole or two, for it was a glorious morning and the course was looking its best.

Everyone else is still asleep, he tells himself. But he is seen from above by an angel who reports what is happening to God, who agrees he should be punished. At the first hole – a par four of over 300 yards – the curate proceeds to hit the drive of his life, and holes out in one.

The angel is confused, saying to God that he thought the offender was to be punished. Instead he had just done something all golfers dreamed of doing – a remarkable hole in one.

'Yes', replied God, 'but who's he going to tell?'

– (contributed by Percy Huggins of *Golf Monthly*).

* * *

The local vicar was a member of the local golf club and usually chose partners from his own age-group and sharing his dignified views. But in the club knock-out he was drawn against a new member – a young upstart who had no idea of dignity. Having disturbed the vicar all the way round by his uncouth manners and general behaviour, the youngster added insult to injury by winning the match on the home green.

'No miracles today, vicar,' said the winner cheerily.

'I cannot work miracles,' replied the vicar gravely, 'but if your parents come to church some time I could marry them.'

* * *

WELL, *DON'T* LISTEN—ANYTHING I HAVE TO SAY IS BETWEEN ME AND THE BALL!

Caddies

Various factors, mainly economic, have conspired to reduce the number of caddies and affect the status and character of those who remain.

Fifty years ago scarcely any golfer went without a caddie and the humblest of clubs would employ a caddie master in charge of a group of local men and boys ready and willing to work for a few shillings a day. The noted centres for golf had large caddie populations, and the majority of the men concerned were full-time regulars. They were professionals at their jobs, often knowing much more about the game than their employers, and in many cases able to play golf with great skill and shrewdness. The best among them became professional golfers. The rest remained caddies and became possessive, masterful and dogmatic when dealing with their masters and their masters' affairs. They were regarded as 'characters' and had the license of court jesters.

Nowadays the caddie population is thin. A number of regulars are to be found at the big courses where caddie masters are still employed, and these carriers are paid very well for the work they do. Most of them travel to all the big tournaments, in many cases attached to certain competitors, so that spectators become accustomed to familiar player-caddie relationships. But the dominant force in each of these partnerships is that of the player; and the modern caddie, although retaining to some extent the proud possessiveness and sense of importance identified with his predecessors, knows his place and behaves with suitable decorum.

This will explain why most of the best stories of caddies belong to a bygone age, when they were almost the principal actors, often hectoring their employers, displaying truculent partisanship and expressing open hostility towards whoever happened to be carrying for the other side.

Two facets of the caddie's character survive. He still tends to be disgruntled if his advice is not taken; and still uses the royal or editorial 'we' in describing the adventures of his side. Which accounts for quite a few of the following stories.

After the Ryder Cup match of 1949 the Americans played in the PGA Match-play championship at Walton Heath. They didn't do at all well, possibly because they were tired or their wives wanted to get to Paris. Or maybe Walton Heath wasn't their kind of course.

This last idea was inspired by remarks passing between Clayton Heafner and his diminutive but knowledgeable caddie, at the start of a practice round.

'What do I take, caddie?' (looking across the road from the first tee).

'Take your two-iron, sir, and play safe.'

At the next hole, as it was then with its stretch of heather across the fairway to catch a long drive:

'Take your two iron, sir, and play safe.'

At the third, with the bunker in the middle of the fairway:

'Take your two iron, sir, and play safe.'

'Hell', said Clayton, turning on his henchman, 'what kind of a golf course is this?'

* * *

Gene Sarazen tells of trying to qualify in one US Open Championship and lifting his head just at the wrong moment. That topped shot cost him his place. Turning to his caddie he said, 'And I prayed hard for that not to happen.'

'I don't know what you do when you pray, boss – but when I pray I keep my head down.'

*   *   *

The player may experiment with his swing, his grip and his stance. It is only when he begins asking his caddie's advice that he gets on dangerous ground (*Sir Walter Simpson, The Art of Golf*).

*   *   *

Golfer at Berkhamsted (carving a huge divot and seeing the ball move about two feet): 'Did you ever see a shot like that, caddie.'

'Well, sir, it were a bit out of the common.'

*   *   *

Gary Player, when new to the American scene, turned up at a tournament to find a shortage of caddies. Gary told the man in charge that he just had to have a really good one for the tournament, and to stress the point he slipped him ten dollars.

Sure enough, when the tournament got under way, a caddie was assigned to Gary. Everything went fine until they reached the sixth hole.

'What do you think the club is?' asked Gary, but the caddie kept quiet.

'How far do you think it is?' said Gary, a little louder.

'I don't know, boss. It looks like a coupla blocks at least.'

*   *   *

A player in Hell bunker at St Andrews was offered a wedge by his caddie but asked for a No 7 iron. 'Ye'll never get oot o' there wi' that,' expostulated the caddie, but the golfer was adamant and, moreover, played a beautiful recovery shot. He turned to the caddie with a smug expression only to hear the gruff comment:

'If ye tak' that club we' ye when ye dee maybe it'll get ye oot o' hell again.'

* * *

Bishop (whose clubs are being carried by an old reprobate noted for his bad language, and warned by the caddie master to say nothing unless spoken to):

'Where did that sod go, caddie?' (meaning the divot).

'Into the bloody bunker', retorted the caddie (meaning the ball) 'and don't fergit you started it.'

* * *

Caddie (entrusted with card and pencil and told to keep the score of a singularly unsuccessful plodder):

'Sorry, sir, I'll have to guess for this hole. I got properly mixed up with the town clock striking twelve.'

* * *

Every conceivable trade, profession or organisation has a golfing society these days, some of them not well-known to caddies.

One morning at a renowned course the caddies engaged were grouped near the first tee.

'Wot's this lot we've got terday, Fred?' asked one.

'Dunno fer sure', replied his mate, 'but I think it's the Licentious victors.'

* * *

Scottish caddies are notoriously dogmatic in their appraisal of golfers and the advice they tender, and this gives rise to many stories.

Like the one about the golfer having an argument with his caddie about the choice of club at a long short hole. He wanted to take a three-iron and the caddie was adamant in favour of a spoon. The golfer had his way and the caddie watched glumly as the ball flew through the air, landed on the green, and ran into the hole.

'What did I tell you?', cried the golfer, turning round with a broad smile.

'Not bad', replied the caddie without change of demeanour, 'but ye'd ha' done better wi' yer spoon.'

* * *

A similar incident on another Scottish course was viewed by the caddie as little short of tragic.

The argument had been lost by the caddie and the ball had gone into the hole.

'I thought as much', he said. 'You should have taken a four-iron. Yon shot's going to cost you an awful lot of money.'

* * *

Perhaps the most astonishing answer to a golfer's question was given by a small boy on the Leatherhead course.

'How far is this hole, boy?' asked a visitor as he stood on the first tee.

'About five miles from Dorking, sir.'

* * *

The caddie had carried for Bernard Gallacher in the morning and was telling his afternoon customer, a 14 handicap amateur, exactly what clubs the professional had used.

'Bernard took a nine iron for this one', observed the caddie.

'Well, you just give me the five-iron,' growled the golfer. And so it went on until they reached the pond hole and the caddie for once was silent.

'Oh, don't stop now', snarled the golfer. 'What did Bernard Gallacher use here?'

'Well, if he'd been you', observed the caddie, 'he'd have used an old ball.'

* * *

Some caddies, not affected by exaggerated ideas of their own omniscience, merely try to be helpful. Like the small boy who, at a very early stage of his career, carried for a skilful but choleric golfer at Harlech. The player's temper rose to such heights that when he three-putted on one green he threw his putter over the hedge.

'That's out of bounds, sir', cried the laddie, anxious to display his local knowledge.

* * *

Why is this kind of story always told of golfers North of the Tweed? A caddie looking for a job attached himself to a likely-looking new arrival who looked him up and down and finally said:

'Are ye' guid at finding golf balls?'

'Rather, sir', replied the lad.

'Well, go out and find one and we'll start.'

* * *

Henry Longhurst likes to tell the story of a member of Walton Heath playing in a friendly match and finding his ball in a hoof mark in the rough.

'That would have been a nasty one in the medal', observed the player to his friend.

' 'E wouldn't 'ave 'ad it in the medal,' confided one caddie to the other.

* * *

A visitor, from ignorance of the course and indifferent play, lost ground on the match in front and received a request from the following players to allow them through.

'Who was that, caddie?', asked the visitor, indicating one of the overtaking players.

'The Captain of the Club, sir', was the reply. 'He's a very good golfer and a real gentleman. Why, he'd even play with you if he couldn't get anybody else.'

* * *

A professional in a tournament was doubtful about the length of his second shot to the last hole and asked his caddie.

'*A three-iron*' *was the prompt reply.*

The professional doubted this, but took the club and hit a perfect shot to the green.

'What made you think I'd get there with a three-iron?' he asked afterwards.

'Because I'd cleaned all the others.'

* * *

Laddie Lucas tells against himself of how he endured a fit of slicing during practice for the Walker Cup match at Pine Valley, USA, where big trees line all the fairways.

At one hole he had a bigger slice than usual and as the ball sailed towards the dark mass of trees he cried: 'Watch it, caddie. Watch it!'

'Ah doesn't watch 'em, sah', said the coloured caddie. 'Ah just listens.'

* * *

The sweet young thing was anxious to win the competition and confided her hopes and fears to her caddie during a practice round. He gave her some advice and she did better, but lay awake that night pondering the problem. Suddenly she realised she had forgotten her professional's injunction to take the club back smoothly without snatching.

As she waited to start the round next day she said to her caddie:

'Do you know, I was thinking about the competition in bed last night and realised I had been snatching the club back instead of taking it back smoothly. If you see me doing that, let me know.'

Sure enough, after doing well for three holes she committed her besetting sin while driving from the fourth tee, and muffed the shot.

'Now, Miss', said the caddie as he walked after her, 'what were we thinking about last night in bed?'

* * *

News had come in ahead of the players that the club champion had tied the course record, and the Secretary waylaid the two caddies to confirm the report.

'Ay, sir', said the champion's caddie, 'we was round in 68 all right and we ought to've been 67.'

'How was that?' asked the Secretary.

'Well, we was driving down the middle all the way and we was splitting the pin wiv our iron shots and everything was going well until we wants a four for the record – and 'e goes and takes three putts.'

The other caddie could not stand this and broke in with: ''Ere, 'old on, Shorty! *We* did this *we* did this and then '*E* takes three putts!'

'That's right', was the belligerent reply. 'I give him the line for his drives and I clubbed 'im to a bloody inch, but I couldn't do 'is putting fer 'im.'

* * *

All that summer the caddie had carried regularly for the same elderly, earnest beginner whose progress was painfully slow, but of great importance to the caddie, who had been promised a bottle of whisky when the magic 100 was broken.

The great day arrived when after many adventures the golfer found himself on the home green having expended 97 strokes. Both were excited for different reasons, and the golfer agitatedly sent his first putt racing ten feet past the hole.

Immediately the caddie dropped the flagstick, picked up the ball and cried excitedly:

'Ye've done it, sir! Ye've done it! Anyone would gie' ye that.'

* * *

One hole at St Deiniol Golf Club, Bangor, in Wales is a sharp dog-leg to the right. The tee shot is blind and if taken with wood will clear a high stone wall and finish out of bounds.

Those who know, writes Mr A Lee-Williams of Torquay in telling this story, take a five-iron from the tee and play the same club again for the second shot.

"My enthusiastic young caddy whispered to me: 'Visiting teams never win this hole, sir'. 'Why not', I asked. 'We never tell them about the out-of-bounds' came the reply."

* * *

The visitor had toiled round a perfectly strange course, taking five hours in the process and accumulating an approximate score of about 180 – approximate because he had lost eleven balls and spent a good deal of time looking for them.

'What should I give my caddie?', he asked the professional.

'Your clubs, sir', was the prompt reply.

* * *

Jimmy Sheridan, whose portrait hangs in the men's bar at Sunningdale Golf Club, was caddie master there during the time that the Duke of Windsor (then Prince of Wales) was a regular player. And Jimmy's attitude to the Prince and his brother was just the same as his attitude towards the other members.

'What course am I playing on today, Sheridan?', asked the Prince one morning.

'The New Course, Sir.'

'But dammit, Sheridan, you know I prefer the Old Course!'

'Ay, Sir, but the New Course is wider.'

* * *

This is also said to have happened at Sunningdale

Two long-haired untidy youths descended from a car with their clubs and buttonholed one of the senior members who was passing.

'Hey', said one, 'are you the caddie master?'

'No, I'm not, answered the member, looking them up and down, 'but I do happen to know he doesn't need any more caddies today.'

* * *

Wallace Gillespie is a modern St Andrews caddie who has something of the character of the talked-of caddies of olden days.

During the Open Championship of 1955 at St Andrews, where Peter Thomson was defending the title, Gillespie gave him the line for his drive to one hole. Thomson drove in the indicated direction, and on coming up to his ball found it lying between two pot bunkers only a few yards apart.

'You didn't give me much room, did you?' observed Thomson.

'Well, you're the Open Champion, aren't you?', retorted Gillespie.

* * *

The Rt Hon Arthur J Balfour, when Prime Minister and in fact during the whole of his Parliamentary life, was a keen golfer, often to be seen in action at North Berwick and St Andrews during the recesses. On one occasion he had a difficult putt from the far left of the pin at the 11th at St Andrews and asked his caddie for the line.

'Hit it half-a-yard tae the left', he was told, but unfortunatcly hit it to the right of the hole and saw the ball run down into the bunker.

'And tae think the bastards are running the country', observed the disgusted caddie to his colleague.

* * *

The peppery old Colonel was given to uttering many oaths in play, and sought to curb this tendency by offering to pay his caddie sixpence for each one that escaped his lips.

This pleased the caddie for two reasons, because he was a professed hater of bad language, and was never averse from adding to his fee in a legitimate manner.

One day at the end of the round the Colonel handed the caddie three-and-six extra.

The caddie carefully counted the money and then looked up.

'Begging yer pardon Sir', he said, 'but I think there's one short.'

'How do you make that out?' demanded the Colonel.

'Well, sir, there was three "damns" going out, two "bloodies" at the 12th where you played three in the bunker, another "damn" at the 14th, a "By God" at the 17th; and then, sir, when you missed that foot putt just now I distinctly heard you say "bugger it" '

* * *

AGREED, IT'S A SHORT COURSE—BUT YOU MUST ADMIT IT'S TOUGH

In and Around the Clubhouse

The Secretary ushered a young man into the lounge and said to a fierce-looking moustachioed member:

'This visitor wants a game, Colonel. Could you possibly give him one?'

With steely eyes peering from beneath bushy eyebrows the Colonel rapped:

'Your school?'

'Eton, sir.'

'Oxford or Cambridge?'

'Oxford, sir.'

'Get a blue?'

'Yes, sir, in my last year.'

'Umph, better late than never. Army or Navy?'

'Army, sir.'

'Guards, I suppose?'

'No, sir, Artillery.'

'Umph. What's your name?'

'Smiffkin-Bones, sir.'

'What, the Smiffkin-Bones of Worcestershire?'

'No, sir, of Staffordshire.'

'Oh, that lot, eh? I'll give you nine holes.'

* * *

From a Club Suggestion Book: We have today played cards with a member of the Committee who smoked three 'cigars' bought from Mrs Lee. They caused considerable comment and annoyance, and enquiries elicited the fact that no other brand was kept in the club. In the interests of members generally can some decent brand be kept? The present ones are unpleasant and unhealthy in a room.

* * *

New member to distinguished elder passing one of the tables in the dining room:

'Are you on the greens committee, sir?'

Elder (with some dignity): 'I am actually Chairman of the *Green* Committee, sir.'

'Well, you're just the chap. Take a look at this watery mess they call cabbage.'

* * *

From the Notice-Board

It is easier to replace the turf than to returf the place.

* * *

Members and visitors are requested not to pick up lost golf balls until they have stopped rolling.

* * *

The course is not meant to be carted away,
So the divots you cut in the course of your play
Should be neatly replaced, by your caddie or you,
With their roots to the earth and their blades to the dew.

* * *

From a Committee Minute:

The condition of the draught beer, which had been the subject of some complaints from members, was looked into thoroughly by the Committee. It was decided the complaints were groundless, for although the first pint or two tended to be cloudy, the beer was excellent right down to the bottom of the barrel.

* * *

And another:

The lengthy investigation of the clubhouse drains has been completed and the trouble traced to the Stilton in the steward's pantry.

* * *

A very old story, as you will judge from the prices:

Golfer (in a letter to the Club Secretary): 'A caddie today insisted on my paying him one shilling for 11 holes, according to the rules, in spite of the fact that Mr S had agreed with *his* caddie that he should carry the two extra holes for twopence. When I left the club I was jeered at by all the caddies. I warned them but they repeated their conduct. I cannot mention names as a whole but my caddie's name is McDonald. If you will suspend the ringleader I will be grateful.'

* * *

A family party from London saw a suitable spot for a picnic just off the Brighton Road and chose a nice flat piece of turf on which to lay out their repast.

From the building behind them a man in plus fours came running.

'What are you doing with our tee?' he exclaimed.

'It ain't yourn', retorted a pert Cockney voice. 'We brought it wiv us all the way from Bermondsey.'

* * *

The eminent lawyer Lord Evershed went to play at a certain Royal Club and drove up to the entrance in a beautiful luxury car. The hall-porter came out to collect the visitor's bag and the introducing member said:

'My guest, Thompson, is Lord Evershed, Master of the Rolls.'

'And a very fine car it is, too,' replied the porter.

* * *

George Houghton in his Golf Addict Among the Irish *tells some delightful stories. One concerns his arrival at one golf course to be faced with a notice* – This Land is Poisoned – *and he enquired about it from the greenkeeper.*

'It's for your dog,' was the reply. 'That is if you have one, which you haven't, and it doesn't matter anyway because we haven't used weed killer for two years.'

* * *

Another Houghton story is of a member of the Killiney club, John Murray, who was pointing out some of the paradoxes of Irish golf.

'Let's see', said John, marshalling his anomalies, 'although Ireland is a republic and a totally independent political unit, we find Irishmen and women playing for Britain against America for the Ryder, Walker and Curtis Cups, and that the selectors wisely chose Joe Carr of Dublin to be Captain of the 1965 Walker Cup team. When Fred Daly from Ulster won the Open in 1947 it was hailed in the London Press as a great British victory. Two years later our Harry Bradshaw tied with Bobby Locke and the British Press claimed that a home player was stemming the overseas invasion. But when poor Harry was slaughtered by Locke in the play-off the same newspapers said "*The Irishman*" *was no match for the* "*Commonwealth player*".'

* * *

Printers' Pie

In the late 1890's golf was beginning to interest the London Press, and to this development we owe the father of all fast-time stories.

Jack White did 75 in his last round of the Open Championship at Royal St George's, Sandwich, and a message was transmitted to a London evening paper: 'White went round in 75 – a record.'

This fell into the hands of a sports sub-editor, ignorant of golf, who caught the 'stop press' box with the intelligence that 'Jack White broke the record at Sandwich, going round in 7 mins 5 secs.

* * *

Ron Heager, Secretary of the Association of Golf Writers, tells of reporting the Silent Night tournament at Pannal, promoted by manufacturers of mattresses; and reading the next morning that the prize-money had been given by 'a well-known Yorkshire betting firm.'

* * *

Jack Wood phoned his story of a Teacher Senior Tournament and downed a much-wanted drink afterwards with some satisfaction at his opening line: 'Sam King, sweet-swinging star of yesteryear . . .'

He felt different the next day when his line in the newspaper read: 'Sam King, street-singing star of yesteryear . . .'

And all that day at the golf club he heard his friends chanting 'Marta'.

* * *

The late Leo Munro got down to write his story after a windy day in the Open Championship.

'Breezy Birkdale . . . he began, pleased with the alliterative start. He was far from pleased the next morning when his story in print, and with the first word in capitals, began: 'Greasy Birkdale . . .'

* * *

Maurice Hart was once credited with the date-line 'Westwood Hoe, Friday.' Shades of Charles Kingsley, Francis Drake – and Defoe?

* * *

One of our colleagues, describing a winning sandwedge shot by Dai Rees in the match-play championship at Walton Heath, was made to state in print that Rees, with the ball lying on a dandelion root, 'took his sandwich and laid it two feet from the hole.'

This led to some amusing observations by leg-pulling friends from someone who wanted to know whether Dai was a vegetarian to the joker who suggested that this was a typical bread-and-butter shot.

* * *

Frank Moran Tells Tall . . .

Frank Moran, President of the Association of Golf Writers, had a newspaper career lasting about 60 years and although now retired he still writes an occasional article for The Scotsman. He has always been much in demand as an after-dinner speaker and as a raconteur has few equals in the world of golf. We are indebted to him for these stories from his repertory:

The Loyal toast had just been drunk at a golf dinner and all was ready for the speechmaking when one of the diners, who had already partaken somewhat freely of the wine, rolled solemnly along to the chairman and shook him by the hand.

'You're not going already?' asked the chairman. 'Oh, no', was the reply, 'I'm just saying good night while I can still see you.'

* * *

The golf club dinner was well under way when a member at the far end of the room rose, raised a nearly-empty glass and said:

'Mr Chairman, I wish to propose *absent friends*, coupled with the name of the wine waiter.'

* * *

The golf club member due to propose the toast of The Guests had imbibed somewhat injudiciously. He was a small man and not much of him was to be seen above the table even when he stood up. After a few incoherent words he disappeared entirely and the Captain, looking down, saw the speaker on the floor.

'Let's tee him up again, Willie', he said to the member on the other side.

* * *

Two golfers, who had done themselves proud at lunch, played four holes before collecting themselves and their thoughts together.

'Hoo do we stan,' Saundy?' asked one.

'I dinna ken, mon', was the cautious reply, 'it's juist a meeracle.'

* * *

A golfer having awful trouble with his driving suspected that his physical condition was the root cause. But his doctor, after a thorough examination, gave him a clean bill of health.

'You're one of the fittest men I've ever examined,' he said.

'Then that's it,' exclaimed the golfer, 'the pro's sold me a bad driver.'

* * *

A golfer, who had spent a considerable time in two or three St Andrews hostelries, after a day's golf clambered into the Aberdeen-London express at Leuchars Junction on his way home to Edinburgh.

In one corner of the compartment was a Salvation Army officer who eyed him with mixed reproach and commiseration. Not a bit abashed the golfer leaned forward confidentially and said, 'And what might your regiment be?'

'I'm in the Army of the Lord', was the stern reply, 'and we're carrying out a missionary campaign against the demon drink. We've driven the Devil from Aberdeen and from Dundee and now we're going to drive him from Edinburgh.'

'Thash right', beamed the golfer, 'keep the blighter headin' South.'

* * *

Sometimes the arguments as to odds which precede a golf match are more keen than the match itself and often influence the result.

'Ay', said one Scottish golfer to a friend recounting his holiday experiences at St Andrews, 'I asked him what handicap he had and he said he was a poor 18 and hadn't touched a club for months. I said I hadn't been on a golf course for a year and was pretty bad wi' lumbago. So we agreed to play for half-a-croon and, believe me or believe me no', I had to dae twa under fowers to beat him.'

* * *